STO

## DO NOT REMOVE
## CARDS FROM POCKET

# EcoZones

# PRAIRIES

## Lynn M. Stone

### Photos by Lynn M. Stone

**ROURKE ENTERPRISES, INC.**
Vero Beach, FL 32964

**Library of Congress Cataloging in Publication Data**

Stone, Lynn M.
  Prairies / by Lynn M. Stone.
    p. cm. — (Ecozones)
  Includes index.
  Summary: Examines the prairie as an ecological niche and describes
the plant and animal life supported there.
  ISBN 0-86592-446-5
  1. Prairie ecology—Juvenile literature.   2. Prairies—Juvenile
literature.   [1. Prairie ecology.   2. Ecology.]   I. Title.
II. Series: Stone, Lynn M.   Ecozones.
QH541.5.P7S76   1989
574.5'2643—dc20                                    89-32744
                                                      CIP
                                                       AC

# CONTENTS

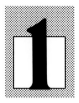

# NORTH AMERICAN PRAIRIE

To the European settlers of North America, the prairie was a whole new world. Accustomed to lands of farms, villages, and forests, they suddenly found themselves in a sea of grass. The vistas of prairie grasses were like nothing they had ever seen before. For some of the early travelers, it was love at first sight. Louis Joliet, in 1673, described the prairie of northern Illinois as country "the most beautiful one can imagine." Author Willa Cather was no less taken with the grassland two hundred years later in Nebraska. She wrote that the prairie was a place of "pure color," where "a gust of wind, sweeping across the plain, threw into life waves of yellow and blue and green."

**Opposite** *Badlands National Park in South Dakota has been sculptured by erosion.*

Once upon a time, the North American prairie sprawled almost unbroken from the edges of the eastern forest west to the Rocky Mountains. It plunged north to the MacKenzie River in Canada where it met the great evergreen forests of the North. It spread south into Texas and northern Mexico and melted, finally, into desert. From north to south

it stretched more than 3,000 miles. When the famous American explorers, Lewis and Clark, reached the Pacific Ocean in 1805, prairies covered more than a million square miles. The heartland of North America was its prairie.

The size of the prairie was breathtaking. Joliet and other French explorers in Illinois, at the eastern edge of the prairie, gazed westward and saw nothing except grassland. Six hundred miles away in Nebraska, two hundred years later, Willa Cather looked around and saw much the same: an ocean of grass rippling in the wind.

PRAIRIES

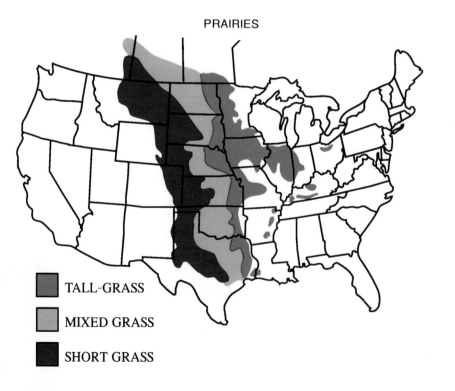

TALL-GRASS

MIXED GRASS

SHORT GRASS

In the passage of time since Lewis and Clark's journey across the continent, the prairie has changed. Much of what used to be prairie has been drained or plowed, built upon, grazed, or planted. But there are still vast remnants of this great inland ocean of grass, especially in the West.

Because it covers so much ground, the prairie, or grassland, is really made up of several different grasslands. The prairies of Illinois and Iowa, for example, are somewhat different than the western prairies of Montana or Colorado. **Ecologists**, scientists who study the interrelationships of plants and animals, have slightly different definitions for prairie. And one ecologist's map of North American prairie may be different from another's. Nevertheless, most ecologists agree that North American prairie is the land covered by native **perennial** grasses and other non-woody plants, such as wildflowers. Perennials are plants that bloom each year from the same root system. Native plants are those that naturally grow in the prairie rather than having been brought to the prairie by man. Between the grasses and the non-woody plants, collectively called **forbs**, it is the grasses that dominated the prairie. Where the grasses begin to be replaced largely by trees, shrubs, or other plants, a transition zone exists. These transition zones, where plants and animals of two or more communities overlap, are often called **ecotones**. Settlers heading westward into Indiana and Illinois found that a thinning of the broadleaf forests began to take place. In these open, park-like woodlands, prairie grasses grew among the bur oaks. The result was a forest-prairie ecotone, a mixing of plant and animal communities.

*Prairie* is the French word for *meadow*. America's grasslands reminded the French explorers of their grassy meadows in France. Meadows and pastures, however, typically are composed of grasses planted by people after the area has been cleared of its original grasses or trees. True prairie, remember, is made up of wild, native plants.

The word *prairie* often brings to mind flat land. Actually, the prairie in much of North America is gently rolling; it is certainly not a flat, unbroken plain. Prairie grasses flow over lumps and hills and into depressions. They rim the little ponds and **potholes** that the **glaciers** dug. Here and there the prairie is channeled by rivers and streams and creased by ravines and canyons.

One of the most striking prairie regions is Badlands National Park in western South Dakota. There the White River has eroded the landscape and left a prairie studded with magnificent, soft-rock sculptures.

Prairies are, indeed, dominated by grasses and non-woody plants. But prairies are by no means entirely tree-less. Trees often flourish along the water courses in otherwise treeless landscapes. They also survive in gullies and, of course, in the transition areas where prairie and forest compete for space.

**Above** *Herd of American bison grazing on mixed-grass prairie in South Dakota.*

9

# TYPES OF PRAIRIE

The true prairie grasslands of North America include a variety of types. Ecologists usually describe three major variations. One is the short-grass prairie close to the Rocky Mountains. Another is the mixed-grass prairie of the central West. The third is the tall-grass prairie of the Midwest. There are other distinct grasslands in the Pacific Northwest, California, the Southwest, Wyoming, northwest Canada, and even Florida. Major grasslands in other countries are the steppes of Eurasia, velds of Africa, pampas of South America, and basalt plains of Australia. For the purposes of this book, *prairie* refers to the traditional and more or less **contiguous** grasslands of midcontinental North America.

The tall-grass prairie is the easternmost grassland. As its name suggests, it is dominated by tall grasses. These include wild rye, cordgrass (sloughgrass), switchgrass, Indiangrass, and especially big bluestem grass.

The historic tall-grass prairie stretched north from Oklahoma eastward into Missouri, Illinois, and western Indiana, and north through Iowa and

**Opposite** *Under stormy dawn clouds, bison graze on mixed-grass prairie.*

Minnesota into Canada's prairie provinces of Manitoba, Saskatchewan, and Alberta. Of all the prairies, the tall-grass has taken the greatest brunt of settlement. Very little of the original tall-grass prairie is left. The fertile black soil of the tall-grass prairie region has become the corn belt of the United States. It is the richest agricultural land in the world.

The grasses of the eastern tall-grass prairie, where they still rustle and wave, have extremely tough, deep-growing roots. Some roots strike 12 feet into the earth.

**Below** *Tall-grass prairie like this one in Kansas once covered much of central United States.*

Among the prairies, the tall-grass was the most lush. The grasses here were taller and denser than on prairies to the west. The black soil was deeper and, as one might expect, the rainfall was the heaviest of the prairie region, approaching 40 inches per year.

West of the tall-grass prairie, rainfall decreases. The soil is less productive, and the native grasses don't grow as tall. This section of middle North America is the mixed-grass prairie. It is a transition zone between the tall grasses of the Midwest and short, sparse grasses that lie just east of the Rocky Mountains.

There are, to be sure, some of the same grass species in the mixed-grass prairies that grow in the tall-grass prairies. They are less robust, however, and they intermingle with other, shorter species from farther west. Typical grasses of the mixed-grass prairie are little bluestem, green needlegrass, needle-and-thread, June grass, and prairie dropseed. Instead of 35 or 40 inches of rain per year, the mixed-grass prairie averages just 23. The soil is drier and the stands of grass look patchier than in the tall-grass prairies. From south to north, the mixed-grass prairie begins in Texas and sweeps north through parts of Kansas, Nebraska, South Dakota, and North Dakota. It includes the southwest corner of Manitoba, southern Saskatchewan, and a small section of Alberta.

Westward, beyond the mixed grasses, the rainfall over grassland diminishes to as few as 15 inches per year. This is short-grass prairie country. The dominant grasses are blue gamma and buffalo grass. Sage plants are numerous and cactus turn up with increasing frequency.

The short-grass prairie blankets portions of western Texas, Oklahoma, Kansas, and Nebraska. It covers much of eastern New Mexico, eastern Colorado, eastern Wyoming, and Montana, with portions of southwest Saskatchewan and southeast Alberta. The short-grass zone is in large measure the work of the Rocky Mountains. The towering Rockies, rising above the plains, intercept rain-laden clouds traveling eastward from the Pacific. As a result, the plains on the east side of the mountains receive comparatively little rainfall, a fact reflected by the short, scattered grasses. The effect of the mountains on rainfall to their immediate east is like the mountains casting a broad shadow in which little rain falls. Scientists refer to this area as the Rockies' rain shadow.

# THE MAKING
# OF THE PRAIRIE

Knowing what the prairie is, recognizing it, and knowing where it is are comparatively easy tasks. Knowing why there is prairie is far more complex, especially where the eastern tall-grass prairie is concerned. Scientists are not quite sure just how the eastern prairie managed to survive in a climate that is just as suited for forest as it is for grassland. After all, there are sections of Illinois, Wisconsin, Indiana, Michigan, and Ohio where prairie and forest stood side by side.

The prairies of the East probably began to develop some time after the last glaciers retreated, 10,000 to 15,000 years ago. The cool, moist air of the time was ideal for the development of evergreen trees—spruces and firs. But the climate became drier. The evergreens vanished and were replaced by trees better suited to a dry climate and by grasses. The grassland of the West, already established, pushed east, sending a peninsula of prairie into Illinois, Ohio, and Indiana.

Fire may also have helped the grasses to gain a foothold. As the old evergreen forests died away, fires could have sealed their fate. If so, the fires would have also hastened the growth of grasses invading from the west. Grasses can usually invade a burned area and establish themselves more quickly than trees.

Fire has been an important element in maintaining prairie as well as establishing it. In the easternmost prairies, trees can live just as easily as grasses. Fires have undoubtedly helped the tallgrass prairie hold out against an invasion of trees. A raging prairie fire only burns the uppermost part of a grass plant. The roots are unharmed, and the plant will spring to life again. The ashes, in fact, act as fertilizer for the grass. The same fire, however, will kill a tree seedling.

Prairie fires have often been started by lightning. The Indians also ignited prairie fires. The fires were useful in stampeding game to a favored killing ground.

Another reason the eastern prairies have maintained themselves is the nature of the grasses themselves. Tall grasses of the eastern prairie form such a deep and extremely tough mat of roots that plants from other communities, such as trees, have a difficult time getting a start. Prairie plants, when they are left alone, can usually squeeze out invader plants. Classic examples of this ability can be seen in the Midwestern states. In Illinois, most of the tall-grass prairie exists only in tiny **relict** patches. Typically, one can find original tall-grass prairie growing along a railroad right-of-way that hasn't been sprayed with plant-killing chemicals (herbicides). Here are tiny slivers of prairie flanked by miles of corn, soybeans, or weeds, yet the native prairie is virtually free of invader plants.

The western prairies are less a mystery. Fire probably has helped them develop, too. But, in addition, the western prairies have developed in dry, windy conditions that favor the growth of hardy grasses rather than trees. Like all plant communities, the prairie, in its various forms, is a product of precipitation, temperature, humidity, soil, and land surface features (topography). Unlike some other plant communities, the prairie has also been shaped by fire.

# 4

# PLANTS OF THE PRAIRIE

The cornerstone of the prairie community is grass. Grasses are the basic fabric of the prairie. Grass is uniquely fit for life in the open. It may be chewed, clipped, trampled, or burned. Grass may be subjected to frigid winters and abrasive winds. Yet grass persists, even prospers.

Grass blades grow upright— vertically. In that way, each blade receives some sunlight without over-shadowing the leaves next to or below it. One acre of grass may have five or ten acres of leaf surface. The greater the leaf surface, the more stored energy the community produces in its plants.

When a leaf is eaten or burned, it grows back up from the roots and soon regains normal size. In periods of extreme heat, cold, or drought, grasses become **dormant**—they temporarily stop growing and trying to use energy that may no longer be available.

Grasses dominate the prairies, but other non-woody plants contribute vegetative cover and also brighten the prairie. The wildflowers of the eastern tall-grass prairies are the most colorful

**Opposite** *July rain on Michigan lilies in tall-grass prairie.*

**Above** *Grasses, like this big bluestem, are the threads that bind the prairies.*

and robust of all the prairie species. Most of the wildflowers are perennials, just as the grasses are. In the prairie it is advantageous for a plant to renew itself each year from the roots rather than have to start from seed. The dense prairie fabric of roots and stems, often called **sod**, makes it difficult for seedlings to take permanent root.

Hundreds of wildflower species are at home on the prairie. For fully seven months of the year the grassland blooms, providing watchers of the prairie with an ongoing wild garden of sometimes riotous color. Each corner of the prairie has its own cast of flowers.

Just which flowers bloom in which corner is governed by such factors as soil type, moisture, and the fall of the land. In low, wet areas, different plants grow than on dry slopes.

Early wildflowers on the tall-grass prairie bloom in late March and April. These early bloomers, such as pasque-flower, shooting star, and white lady's-slipper orchid, are subtle. They grow close to the ground, nearly hidden in the plant litter of the previous season. The grasses are still dormant or short, so the early wildflowers have little competition. The spring blossoms wither quickly, but the plants continue to grow

**Above** *Pasque flowers are among the first wild-flowers to bloom each spring on the tall-grass prairie.*

21

in the shade provided by the next wave of flowers and the growing sprouts of grass.

Each seasonal generation of wildflowers is generally taller than the next. Most prairie flowers tend to be sun-loving. Each plant needs to stand tall enough to catch a shore of sunlight. Mid-summer flowers, like prairie clover, black-eyed Susan, and Michigan lily, are much taller than the spring flowers. Many late summer flowers, competing with the grasses, are taller still.

By late August and September, the tall-grass prairie is ablaze with plumes of gayfeather, towering yellow composites, blue asters, and waves of purple-and-bronze big bluestem. Crouched among the taller blades and stems are blue gentians of several **species**.

Shorter days and autumn frosts herald the end of the growing season. The last of the gentians fade from blue to brown. Leaves of prairie dock, like great, dry elephant ears, crackle in the wind. Soon, parchment-dry and lifeless, the prairie will slumber through another winter.

**Opposite** *Purple prairie clover enlivens mid-summer tall-grass prairies.*

# 5 ANIMALS OF THE PRAIRIE

Before the prairies were settled, wild animals were abundant on the grasslands. In South Dakota, Captain Meriwether Lewis of the Lewis and Clark expedition wrote, "This scenery, already rich, pleasing, and beautiful, was still further heightened by immense herds of buffalo, deer, elk, and antelopes, which we saw in every direction, feeding on the hills and plains. I do not think I exaggerate when I estimate the number of buffalo which could be comprehended at one view to amount to three thousand." The disappearance of the great herds of buffalo and other grazing animals has certainly changed the impression of the prairie since the time of Captain Lewis. Nevertheless, many prairies are still a source of plentiful wildlife.

In any community of wild plants and animals, much of the animal activity occurs out of sight. This is especially true on the prairies. Many animals live at least part of their lives underground or hidden in the dense *swales* of grass and flowers. And not all of the prairie animals, of course, are the size of buf-

**Opposite** *Sandhill cranes and other migratory water birds gather on prairie marshes.*

falo. The little animals without backbones, the invertebrates, are everywhere on the prairie, but they are best seen by keen-eyed observers.

Some of the most common invertebrates of the prairie are insects. One of the most important of these is the grasshopper. Grasshoppers, which feed directly on plants, sometimes build their populations to 30 per square yard. Not as common, but much more pleasing to see, are butterflies, which are attracted by the ongoing parade of wildflowers. Prairies are a favorite haunt of such species as monarch, fritillary, and swallowtail.

**Below** *The monarch is one of many butterfly species that visit prairie wildflowers.*

Reptiles and amphibians are not easily seen on the prairies either. Like many other prairie animals, they tend to occupy burrows or, in the case of amphibians, hide in the mud of prairie pools or potholes. Toads and tiger salamanders are among the common amphibians that live in and near prairie wetlands and ponds.

Several snakes, many of which prey on rodents, are found almost exclusively in prairies. Two of the harmless varieties are the bullsnake and the smooth green snake. Two poisonous snakes of the prairies are the prairie rattlesnake and the eastern massasauga, a smaller rattler.

**Above** *The prairie rattlesnake hunts rodents on the western prairies.*

Turtles, like snakes, are reptiles. Several species of turtles live in prairie streams and rivers. But one turtle actually lives on dry land in the prairie grass. This is the ornate box turtle, an attractive little creature whose lower shell, called a plastron, has a hinge. While pond and river turtles can retract their heads, the box turtle can retract its head and also tightly close its bottom shell against its top shell. The ornate box turtle is well-adapted to prairie life. Its shell offers full-time protection against predators, and it never goes hungry. It eats berries, grass, insects, and nearly everything else it can find. In cold or hot weather, the box turtle burrows underground.

The prairie grasses hide several ground-nesting birds. Meadowlarks, bobolinks, Henslow's sparrows, vesper sparrows, grasshopper sparrows, and horned larks are among the songbirds that nest on the prairie. Short-eared owls and many shorebirds, such as the marbled godwit, also nest in the prairie grass. Burrowing owls nest under the prairie, usually in the abandoned burrow of a badger or ground squirrel.

Water birds are associated with prairie ponds and marshes. Ducks of many species and the giant Canada

goose often nest in the grass near a marsh or pond. Grebes build floating nests of marsh vegetation. Huge white pelicans lay their eggs on the islands of prairie lakes. Double-crested cormorants and gulls share islands with the pelicans.

No prairie view is complete without a bird of prey circling lazily or diving toward its prey. For open field hunters, like marsh hawks, rough-legged hawks, red-tailed hawks, prairie falcons, and golden eagles, the prairie is a banquet table of rodents. Turkey vultures,

**Above** *White pelicans feed their young on islands shared with cormorants and gulls.*

29

another of the birds of prey, are not hunters, but they are quick to clean up, or **scavenge**, the leftovers of the hunters.

Most birds use the prairie for only part of the year. With the onset of autumn and the scarcity of many foods, the majority of birds migrate south for the cold months. Great clouds of ducks and geese, most of them from the Far North, take brief refuge on prairie ponds, lakes, and rivers. In Nebraska each fall, waves of sandhill cranes rest along the Platte River.

One bird that does make the prairie its year-round home is the prairie chicken. The prairie chicken is a member of the grouse family. The chicken is only a distant relative. Prairie chickens are among the most fascinating animals of the grassland. Each spring, on chilly, pre-dawn mornings, the males gather on "dancing grounds" or *leks*. To win a female's favor, the males strut, jump, drum their feet in a blur, and spar with each other. During these courtship rituals, they inflate air sacs like yellow balloons on each side of their heads.

In a sea of vegetation, it is no wonder that rodents and other plant-eating mammals are abundant on the prairie. Mice and their relatives, the

voles, live in tunnels and grass-lined passages. Several kinds of ground squirrels live in the burrows they dig. One of the ground squirrels goes by a most inappropriate name—prairie dog.

Prairie dogs and the other ground squirrels, because of their digging activities, help loosen, aerate, and mix the prairie soil. In effect, the ground squirrels plow the soil and enrich it.

Unlike its relatives, the prairie dog is a very sociable animal. In the 1800s, some prairie dog "towns" were reported to cover thousands of square miles and contain millions of prairie dogs. Today

**Above** *Prairie chicken males impress their mates each spring by inflating air sacs while they "dance."*

31

**Above** *Prairie dogs live in sprawling "towns" of burrows on the western prairies.*

the prairie dog towns of the mixed- and short-grass prairies are tiny by comparison.

Prairie dogs like a clear view; they keep the grass near their burrows clipped. The low grass and burrow mounds of prairie dog villages are attractive to bison, which love to roll and wallow in the dirt.

Of all prairie animals, probably none is as symbolic of, and well suited to, the prairie as the American bison or buffalo. Buffalo can endure cold, heat, and drought. Furthermore, they can run, swim, and drive off any attacker except man.

When there were still buffalo without number, they sometimes overgrazed an area, just as cattle will do today. (Buffalo eat tremendous amounts of grass.) But they moved on, and the overgrazed area eventually replenished itself. At one time there may have been as many as 60 million buffalo in North America. Today, all of the plains buffalo, which number in the thousands, are in American or Canadian preserves and parks.

Mammals of the prairie can typically run or burrow. Those survival skills are called **adaptations**. Animals of any community develop certain adaptations that allow them to survive in that community. A squirrel's ability to climb, for instance, is not useful in the open prairie, but it is an essential adaptation for life in the forest. Many prairie mammals, such as the ground squirrels, can burrow. Another useful adaptation to life on the prairie is speed. Jackrabbits, deer, and pronghorn antelope depend upon speed for their survival.

The pronghorn is the fastest land animal in North America. For three or four minutes it can bound along at up to 60 miles per hour. It has excellent eyesight, too, another adaptation for life in the open. Pronghorns are grazers, like bison and prairie dogs. They avoid competition with bison by eating many weedy plants that don't appeal to bison.

The dominant meat-eating animals of the prairies used to be grizzly bears and wolves. The **races** of grizzlies and wolves that lived on the western prairies are gone; they were shot, trapped, and poisoned into extinction long ago. Today in the western states, cougars may occasionally prowl the grassland, but they prefer mountain and forest. In the absence of cougars, wolves, and bears, coyotes are the largest predators of the grassland. Other meat-eating animals of the grassland are badgers, long-tailed weasels, the rare kit fox, and

**Below** *Bison bull snorts while the dust settles back into its prairie wallow.*

the even rarer black-footed ferret.

Not all of the animals in a prairie are necessarily always bound to grassland. The prairie chicken is. It depends on the food and safety of the grassland; nothing else suits it as well, and it cannot fly long distances. But many other animals, like the red-tailed hawk and mule deer, can and do use other types of natural communities.

**Above** *Once counted in the millions, American bison are now restricted to herds in parks and reserves.*

# THE FLOW OF ENERGY

The prairie is a community, a home in which several plants and animals share common needs. Each plant and animal in the community has a niche, a particular role to play in the welfare of the community. Through these various plants and animals, from one to another, food is passed along. With the food goes energy needed to live.

The first building block of the prairie community and the transfer of energy is the sun. Through a series of complex reactions, sunlight helps green prairie plants convert nutrients from the soil and air into food. A key process is called **photosynthesis**, and it nourishes the plant.

**Opposite** *The conversion of sunlight into food by prairie plants is basic in the flow of energy.*

Because plants produce basic food and energy, they are called **producers**. The food and energy they contain is transferred from one organism to another when each one eats and is eaten. This passage of food and energy from one animal to another is called a **food chain**. A grasshopper, for example, feeds directly upon the prairie grass. In doing so, the grasshopper unlocks the foods stored in the blade of grass. The

**Above** *Pronghorns are herbivores; they eat and take their energy from plant material.*

grasshopper becomes a **consumer**, an animal that depends upon the energy stored in other living things. When the grasshopper is eaten, perhaps by a green snake, the energy moves again along the chain. The green snake, in turn, may be eaten by a coyote or fox. Within the prairie community are countless food chains. One animal may be part of several. Together, as they interact, the chains are called a **food web**.

Some animals, then, such as the grasshopper, bison, and pronghorn, are strictly **herbivores**, plant eaters. Others are meat eaters, or **carnivores**. These include the golden eagle, coyote, and kit fox. Others, such as the box turtle, are omnivores; they eat both plant and

animal material. But in all cases, the flow of energy can be traced back through chains of consumers to green plants.

The cycle of energy moving from plants to large animals is completed by *decomposers.* Decomposers are the plants and animals that break dead tissue down into simple chemical compounds. When a buffalo or coyote dies, the animals that feed off the carcass begin the processes that return the carcass to the soil. Eventually, green plants will be able to use nutrients that were once part of the buffalo. First, the buffalo is reduced by such decomposers as insects and bacteria into the simple forms that become part of the soil.

# 7 PRAIRIE CONSERVATION

Over thousands of years a natural bargain was struck. The prairie plants ripened in the sun. The plant eaters and the meat eaters ate their fill. In a complex web of food chains, energy flowed with the supply and demand in balance. The Indians were never numerous enough to tilt the balance or scar the prairie. In fact, their frequent torching of the grasses helped the prairie to renew itself each spring.

But in less than a century, the prairie community was changed for all time. Change began in the eastern prairies. John Deere's steel plow provided a new-found way of breaking through the tough prairie sods. Prairie grass disappeared, replaced by rows of corn and beans. By the early 1900s the tall-grass prairie had been converted into America's corn belt.

*Opposite A tall-grass prairie remnant in Illinois glistens in early morning light.*

Settlement spread westward after the Civil War in 1865. The trickle of pioneers who had followed Lewis and Clark became a torrent. The U.S. Army, no longer saddled with the threat of the Confederacy, turned its attention to the plains Indians and their lifeblood, the

bison. The "hostile" Indians were either destroyed or confined to reservations. The buffalo were slaughtered. Much of the prairie was rapidly settled by pioneers.

The pioneers were quick to change their surroundings. Crops replaced buffalo grass. The grizzlies, elk, wolves, trumpeter swans, and whooping cranes were hunted to near-extinction. Thousands, perhaps millions, of prairie dogs were poisoned because they competed with hungry cattle. And by 1900 the untold millions of plains buffalo had dwindled to a last wild band of 20. Fortunately, another 500 or so had been huddled away in zoos and private herds. These privately owned bison were the ancestors of most of our buffalo today.

The tall-grass prairies were especially hard-hit because of their unrivaled soil. Of 400,000 square miles of original tall-grass prairie in North America, less than one percent, fewer than 4,000 square miles, remains. So little tall grass remains in Illinois, the "prairie state," that most of the millions of people in the prairie state have never seen prairie.

The mixed-grass and short-grass prairies have fared better. Much of the western prairie was never plowed. Rather, it was used for cattle ranching, and prairie can coexist with cattle reasonably well if the cows are not grazed to excess.

The prairie in many places is gone, part of another time. Here and there, however, like scattered pieces of a jigsaw puzzle, bits of original prairie survive. In some states, which still have large prairie tracts, a new, rising interest in protecting prairie may help ensure that some of those prairie tracts will be saved for all time. Meanwhile, in those wondrous places of grass and sun and sky, badgers still loot prairie dog towns and shorebirds weave hidden nests in grassy, green tangles.

# GLOSSARY

**adaptation**   a characteristic of function, form, or behavior that improves an organism's survival chances in a particular habitat

**carnivores**   meat-eating animals

**consumer**   an animal, in the context of having to eat, or consume, to live

**contiguous**   in actual contact, or touching

**dormant**   a state of inactivity due to the slowing or stopping of normal functions

**ecologist**   a scientist who studies the interrelationships of plants and animals in association with their environment

**ectotone**   a transition zone in which plants and animals of two or more communities overlap

**food chain**   the transfer of energy from green plants through a series of consuming animals

**food web**   the network of interlocking food chains

**forb**   grasses and other non-woody green plants, such as wildflowers

**glacier**   a massive river of ice that forms on high ground when snowfall exceeds summer melting

**herbivores**   plant-eating animals

**perennial**   a plant that blooms each year from the same root system

**photosynthesis**   the process by which green plants produce simple food sugars through the use of sunlight and chlorophyll

**pothole**   a depression, often circular and water-filled, gouged by a glacier

**producer**   a green plant, in the context of its ability to manufacture, or produce, food

**race**   variations within an animal species, usually with regard to size, color, and preferred habitat

**relict**   an area left unchanged after similar areas around it have been altered or destroyed

**scavenge**   to clean up food scraps

**sod**   the dense fabric of roots and stems in the earth

**species**   a group of plants or animals whose members reproduce naturally only with other plants or animals of the same group; a particular kind of plant or animal, such as an American bison or fringed gentian

# PRAIRIE SITES

The following is a list of sites where you can expect to find characteristic plants and animals of the prairies:

## CANADA

**Alberta**
Cypress Hills Provincial Park, northwest of Medicine Hat, Alberta
Dinosaur Provincial Park, northeast of Brooks, Alberta
**Manitoba**
Riding Mountain National Park, north of Brandon, Manitoba
**Saskatchewan**
Prince Albert National Park, northwest of Prince Albert, Saskatchewan

## UNITED STATES

**Illinois**
Goose Lake Prairie State Park, Morris, Illinois
**Indiana**
Indiana Dunes National Lakeshore, Chesterton, Indiana
**Iowa**
Union Slough National Wildlife Refuge, Titonka, Iowa
**Kansas**
Konza Prairie Preserve, Manhattan, Kansas
**Missouri**
Taberville Prairie, St. Clair, Missouri
**Montana**
Bowdoin National Wildlife Refuge, Malta, Montana
Custer Battlefield National Memorial, Crow Agency, Montana
Medicine Lake National Wildlife Refuge, Medicine Lake, Montana
**Nebraska**
Crescent Lake National Wildlife Refuge, Ellsworth, Nebraska
Fort Niobrara National Wildlife Refuge, Valentine
Valentine National Wildlife Refuge, Valentine
**North Dakota**
Arrowhead National Wildlife Refuge, Kensal, North Dakota
Des Lacs National Wildlife Refuge, Kenmare, North Dakota
Lower Souris National Wildlife Refuge, Upham, North Dakota
Theodore R. Roosevelt National Park, Medora, North Dakota
Upper Souris National Wildlife Refuge, Foxholm, North Dakota
**Oklahoma**
Wichita Mountains National Wildlife Refuge, Fort Sill, Oklahoma
**South Dakota**
Badlands National Park, Interior, South Dakota
Custer State Park, Custer, South Dakota
Samuel H. Ordway Memorial Prairie, Aberdeen, South Dakota
Wind Cave National Park, Hot Springs, South Dakota
**Wisconsin**
University of Wisconsin Arboretum Prairie, Madison, Wisconsin
Crex Meadows Prairie and Wildlife Area, Grantsburg, Wisconsin
**Wyoming**
Yellowstone National Park, Wyoming

# ACTIVITIES

Here are some activities and projects that will help you learn more about the North American prairies:

1. Choose one of the prairie states or provinces. Find out where prairie is protected in that state or province. Use the state or provincial department of conservation or natural resources for help in obtaining your information.

2. Choose a prairie animal and tell how it is specially made (adapted) for life in the prairie environment.

3. Draw a map of North America and show the extent of prairie. Illustrate your map with drawings or pictures of typical prairie plants and animals such as bluestem grass, pronghorns, prairie dogs, and bison.

4. Draw a prairie food chain or several prairie food chains, showing the relationships of sunlight to plants, plants to animals, animals to animals.

5. Report on one of the major prairie reserves in the United States or Canada. (See the list in this book for ideas.) Write to the appropriate park for information.

6. If you have access to a prairie, take a series of photographs of prairie plants and seasons. Arrange your photos on posterboard or in a scrapbook to show the changes that occur on the prairie.

7. Write an essay in which you tell why the prairie should be protected, or an essay that tells "how much a prairie is worth."

8. Create a collage of prairie plants and animals.

9. Join a conservation organization that promotes prairie protection and restoration. Several national organizations are listed here:

Defenders of Wildlife
1244 Nineteenth St., NW
Washington, DC 20036

National Audubon Society
Membership Data Center
P.O. Box 2666
Boulder, CO 80322

National Wildlife Federation
1412 Sixteenth St., NW
Washington, DC 20036

The Nature Conservancy
1800 N. Kent St.
Arlington, VA 22209

Sierra Club
730 Polk St.
San Francisco, CA 94109

# INDEX

Numbers in boldface type refer to photo pages.